Times Yet To Be

Jarrod Brown, DDS, DWS

Dedication

For Dad, Mema, and Papa
and everyone I love,
Especially
Mom, Lisa, Trevor and Nathan

Contents

JARROD BROWN, DDS, DWS

Introduction and Acknowledgements

Until I became a father, I didn't realize that you could learn a spiritual lesson from refrigerator magnets. More specifically, alphabet magnets. But God finds a way to speak His word into most anything we encounter. Thus, this collection of poetry.

At breakfast one day when he was four, my son, Trevor, looked at the magnets and said, "Hey Daddy, I think I can spell the word 'map.'" So I encouraged him to get up from the table and try. He went to the refrigerator, picked up the letters M A and P, and correctly spelled map. Needless to say I was a proud Papa. But then I looked above the word MAP and saw that another proud Papa was speaking to me. Above MAP was spelled out the word BIBLE. And, obviously, God was teaching me that the Bible is our map to Him. "Out of the mouths of babes...."

As I began this book of poetry, I sensed that God spoke to us through many situations, through nature, and through the seasons of the Christian year in ways that I had never considered. So I endeavored to construct through poetry some of the emotions, sensations, revelations, and joys that we experience in and out of our relationship with Christ: to show an average "year in the life" of yours truly. I found myself intrigued that we as humans have compartmentalized the things we enjoy by where they fall on the calendar and how they relate to certain holidays and holy days. For example, we might feel pride in our country all year round, but especially it seems to burst forth around the official holidays of Memorial Day and Fourth of July. Similarly, we as Christians attempt to live out the principles of hope, peace, joy, and love all year, although they truly manifest themselves in our actions during the seasons of Advent and Christmas.

I have always said that as one plans services of worship, one must endeavor to reach all people, at all ages, at all stations of life, at all levels of education and understanding. I have tried to do the same with this collection of poetry. I have adopted different styles, some more simple and obvious than others, to reach every level of understanding. Some are geared toward children, while others appeal more toward those of us who have lived awhile longer. In essence, I have tried to emulate the Apostle Paul, whose goal it was to be "all things to all people" in order to reach them with the Gospel. I hope I have been successful.

My only request to you, dear reader, is that you try to put yourself in my place as you read these poems. You will likely find yourself in many word pictures, and then again you may experience some adventures you never expected. Just remember that God created this world for all of us to enjoy, and sent His Son so that we might have a relationship with Him. If you come away from this book understanding this idea, then you have understood my reason for writing these verses.

No one ever completes a book of poetry, prose or anything else without the assistance of many other people. So it is with me. I am so thankful to my wife Lisa, whom I love dearly, for her encouragement to me to take time away from our busy lives raising Trevor and Nathan to finish this book. I also would like to thank my friend and fellow writer, Cindy Morgan Brouwer, for her ability to help me see things from a different point of view and for suggesting several of the subjects found within this book. I also give thanks, posthumously, to Robert E. Webber for inviting me to be a student at the school he founded, the Institute for Worship Studies that now bears his name. In that "ruinous work" I truly found my place in God's kingdom and came to understand that the story of God is central to our understanding of and relationship with Him. I am thankful for my professors there, Drs. Jim Hart, Andy Hill, Lester Ruth, Jack Van Marion, Reggie Kidd, Constance Cherry, and our Dean of the Chapel, Darrell Harris, for their deep contribution to my spiritual development and understanding of Church history and worship. Of equal importance to me are my readers and editors, Dr. K. Porter Aichele, Dr. Chris Brewer, and Dr. Mary Jane Brewer, and Darrell A. Harris, who each helped me to refine the language and imagery of this book. Thanks also to Rev. Joshua Hearne for his help in both editing and laying out this book for publication and for his leadership in our town in the area of homelessness and near-homelessness. Next to last, I am grateful to my mother, Judi, my Aunt Mary Bray, my "sisters from another mister" Sherri Katoen and Ingrid McCraw and my brothers Maurice Katoen and Dale McCraw, for their prayer support during this huge undertaking. Finally, and most importantly, I thank my Savior, Jesus Christ, for the hope, peace, joy, and love He has brought to my life over our last 44 years together. I am especially grateful for His eternal care of all my loved ones who have gone home before me, especially my father, Jackson, my "Mema," Lucile Motley and my "Papa," Gilmer Motley. I dedicate this book to their memory and in thanksgiving for all the love and support they showed me in life and still give me in the "great cloud of witnesses." I love you all.

My very best wishes to you, dear reader, as you savor all of your "Times Yet To Be."

Jarrod Brown, DDS, DWS
27 January 2016
Sweetpea Hill, Danville, Virginia

1 Winter

New Year

Beginning again a chart of days
Some with hardship, many with praise.
Thinking ahead to plans we may make,
And worrying which of those plans we will break.
Dreaming ahead of the times yet to be:
Easter, and Christmas, and days by the sea,
Weight to be lost and foods yet to try,
Loving the ones we have 'ere we die,
Sunshine and snow, windstorms and rain,
Umbrellas up and quickly down again,
Springtime flowers and autumn leaves,
Shorts and flip-flops and long sweater sleeves.
The days still to come are each a new journey,
Each with new hope and new songs to be learning,
Special times of worship and days set for rest,
Birthdays, and parties, and all of life's best.
And each day is perfect for worshiping God
Giving thanks to Him for all He has wrought,
For without Him the future would be very drear,
But loving dear Jesus gives us peace for the year.

~~Jarrod Brown, DDS, DWS, 4 January 2016

Sing Up the Son

Sing up the sun:
Let break of day be lauded
With chirruping and huzzahs,
Birdsong and human harmony,
As blackness gives way
To deep purple, then lilac and grey
Before bright oranges and azure blues
Flood God's world with love light.

Sing up the Son:
Let the one and only Begotten
Be given first place in the morning
That he so diligently created,
Empowering every tweet and twitter,
Voice and victory,
Since before the dawn of men.

Sing up the sun,
And give thanks for one more breath,
One more view of the world,
One more visit with family and friends.
One more chance to set things aright,
To strengthen mind and body,
To participate in the dance of life.

Sing up the Son,
Who gives each breath
And made the world to praise Him
And visits us through family, friends,
And ultimately, faith,
Give thanks to Him who made things right
By giving His holy body,
To give us everlasting life.

Sing up the sun,
For morning breaks.
Sing up the Son,
For the Morningstar breaks through.
A new day to see Him,
A new life to serve Him,
Beast, bird, saint, and sunrise:
Sing up the Son.

~~Jarrod Brown, DDS, DWS, 12 December 2015

Epiphany acrostic

Eastern magi
Peruse the stars
In search of Messiah.
Packing their camels
Hurrying to Judea
And finding Him born.
Now they sense freedom:
Yearning for God is fulfilled.

~~Jarrod H Brown DDS, DWS, December 18, 2014

Winter View

Sitting by the window pane
I look outside on cold and rain
And wonder if this falling mist
By icy breath will soon be kissed
And change itself to ice and snow,
Which, as all the children know,
Will make a wonderland for play:
A snowman-making, sledding day.
With drifts of white so very deep
That trudging through entices sleep
And freezes tiny little toes
And rosies each and every nose.
Mother, inside, will not go out
And so will rush the pantry out.
She'll cook a soup so very warm,
That after admiring Frosty's charm,
Everyone will run inside to eat
Leaving piles of gloves on the window seat.
How I'll miss those days of little boys
And all their snowball-throwing joys,
Of screams and laughs and hullabaloo
Of bluish lips and chattering chews.
These winter memories I'll carry true
In my middle age and dotage, too,
For this winter view has shown me life:
The love of children, home, and wife.

~~Jarrod Brown, DDS, DWS, 15 January 2016

Behold the Lamb of God

Hairy man preached repentance
In the middle of the river
Surrounded by dirty sinners
And the one man without sin.

Waters washed the camel hair
And drenched his leather belt,
Reminding him of leather sandal straps
That he was not worthy to loose.

But on the riverbank
The one man shed his own shoes
And walked into the river unafraid,
Unashamed and undoubting of his task.

The hairy man stumbled back on a rock
Nearly falling in the deep rush
"Behold the Lamb of God,"
The Lamb that was also his cousin.

And the one man lowered himself
Beneath the flood he himself created,
Lowered himself as a man in need of a wash
And his cousin was frozen stiff by the sight.

Overhead, in purest shining white
A dove of his own creation
Fell as a feathered arrow from heaven
And gently perched on his soaking shoulder.

And the terrible voice that created all things
Boomed from the outer limits of space
So that none could be mistaken:
"This is my beloved Son."

The Son heard and worshiped his Father,
The cousin in amazement worshiped his Father-cousin,
The people trembled in awe and voiced the ancient question:
"Could he be the one?"

~~Jarrod Brown DDS, DWS, 31 October 2015

Wedding at Cana

Partygoers perplexed
Vintage vanished
Groom aghast
Guest guesses
Mother moves
Son suspicious
Mother mentions
Son sermonizes
Mother mandates
Son surrenders
Miracle amazes
God glorified
Power presented
Son singled out
Mission embarks.
    ~~Jarrod Brown DDS, DWS, 13 December 2015

Transfiguration

In a mountaintop experience
Ancient prophecy is brought to light
And the deity of the Son of Man is glorified.
Powerfully smitten, the head disciple
Expresses his desire to make camp
And stay forever in the eternal sunshine.
But the point is truly received
When the light is overshadowed,
And in the fog of loss and confusion,
The Voice speaks:
"This is My beloved Son! Hear Him!"
And in that same fog, not in the light,
Belief dawns for three men.
But not so for the rest of the world.
Not yet.
For the gift of God
Is treated with utter contempt:
Utter ruin and devastation come to Him
In another mountaintop experience.
But out of the darkness of death,
The Light shines anew,
And belief dawns for all
Who will hear and believe
The Voice crying out:
"It is finished."

~~Jarrod Brown, DDS, DWS, 4 January 2016

Ash Wednesday

Last year's palms shouted Hosannas,
This year they are burned to ash.
Holy oil is added and the mixture sanctified:
A waving acclamation becomes a sooty mash.

The prophets and the Gospel books
Are opened and to us sinners present
A call to return our lives to God
And to seek Him through a holy Lent.

Prayers, litanies, and gifts of absolution
Remind us that Christ's work is done,
That nailing our sins upon His Cross,
The Son, for us, forgiveness has won.

A reminder of our sinful past,
That from dust to dust our lives run,
The blackened ash crosses upon our brows
Show the grace and love of God's Son.

In prayer and deep repentance
We leave to fast and pray,
To give pure alms and deny ourselves
In Christ's Name for forty purple days.

~~Jarrod Brown, DDS, DWS, 22 January 2016

Lent (Forgiving Alms Prayer acrostic)

Forgiving ourselves and others
As Christ has forgiven us;
Saving ourselves from worldliness
To be able to serve others
Is the point of our Lenten fast:
Not spending what we want and
Giving to others what they need.

Among us always are the poor
Left to us by Christ to show our care:
Money, time, relationship building,
Serving them as we have been served.

Praise and adoration,
Requests made for those near and far,
Always giving thanks for what we have,
Yearning to hear from God,
Eager to follow His direction,
Reaching out to others with His love.

~~Jarrod Brown, DDS, DWS, 22 January 2016

Lament

Why do I wander away from Your presence, Lord,

When Your Spirit has manifested Himself so clearly and richly?

Why is my nature such that I turn to baser things rather than those things that please You, than to those things that glorify Your Name?

I rival Paul in the list of chief sinners, but rather than keeping on the road of repentance, I take a sharp left turn to the avenue of sin and death.

You have provided me every ease and every favor, yet I spit on your hospitality.

I am lower than an accursed slave who will not obey his Master.

Though You reprove me, and I do not obey, Your love for me never ceases.

The weight of your love, O Lord, is more than I can bear

And insomuch your Son bore it for me.

In my twists and turns You are yet guiding me;

Your Morning Star shines in the distance.

The depths of the sea and the vault of the sky cannot contain Your love for me,

And so it rains down upon my fields yielding a good
harvest, in spite of my poor husbandry.

I cannot steer the plow on my own,

So You yoke me together with brothers and sisters
whose burden I also make lighter.

When will I learn to hear Your voice,

In the soft chiding and gentle encouragement of my
fellow travelers?

It is a sound I cannot search out and cannot live without;

Your voice is soft violin and strumming guitar in my
untrained ear.

Do not cease Your Song over me, Gentle Savior,

For your song in the night is my Evenstar

And your morning hymn is my sword and shield.

Direct me in Your music, Lord, and sing peace into my
soul;

Make me a river of Your love that flows into the sea of
faith;

Change me from a slave to an obedient servant

And lead me to life again.

~~ Jarrod Brown, DDS, 5 July 2006

St. Patrick

Bright green in a midst of purple time,
Time to enjoy rather than to fast,
To recall the shepherd of God who
Helped Irish faith to flourish and last.
A driver of snakes,
If any there were,
And a user of nature
To explain God to curs:
Three leaves in a shamrock,
In everlasting green
That point to the Trinity,
One true God in Three.
A symbol of power,
Of heavenly life,
Whose vivid green hue
Pierces hearts like a knife.
A slave to men
And even to priests,
Patrick brought Christ
To the bold and the least.
May his example
Inspire us to share
The goodness of God
To wee folk everywhere.

~~Jarrod Brown, DDS, DWS, 16 January 2016

2 Spring

Wispy Visions

Fluffy grey elephants lead the parade
Across the blue-grey canvas above,
And plump little geese follow behind
The circus train that they love.
Dragonish creatures blow out billows
As schooner ships sail away,
And sunlight lends rainbow color
To all the wispy visions today.
Powered by the gusty gales
Poufs and pillows push by,
Changing carelessly
To whatever pleases my eye.
Springtime is here,
And the grasses are lush.
Today I dally to stare above
For Tomorrow may call me to rush.

~~Jarrod H Brown, DDS, DWS, 20 April 2015

Cartwheels

He went to bed
Tomorrow was just another day
A day of hard breathing
A day of hard walking
But God was with Him.
He woke up
And it was still the same night
A night of hard thinking
A night of hard walking
What was God doing?
He cried out
And the love of his life ran out
The time had come
The time was over
And God took him.
He woke up
And it was eternal day
A day of easy breathing
A day of easy walking
And God did cartwheels with him down the golden
street.

~~Jarrod Brown DDS, DWS, January 16, 2015, in
memory of my father, Jackson

Spring is Here

Green onions amongst the greening grass,
Pink blossoms on the cherry trees,
Daffodils and crocus burst from the ground,
And all around is heard the buzzing of bees.
Spring is here.
Robins and cardinals build up their nests
And steal worms to feed their young.
Warmer breezes blow new leaves
That the trees from their branches have hung.
Spring is here.
April rains refresh the hardened soil,
Allowing May flowers to shoot through,
While cotton-tailed bunnies hop through the yard,
And kids hunt for Easter eggs, too.
Spring is here.
Year after year the drear winter is defeated
And Spring puts on her colorful show,
Bringing us hope and a smile on our face
For God has not forgotten His own.
Spring is here.
At last.

~~Jarrod Brown DDS DWS, 25 March 2015

Sing the Song of Spring

Sunlight shines on my shoulder
Through wide windows of grainy green glass
Reminding me that Spring has sprung:
Time to wade in wild, wavy green grass.
But business beckons and patients petition,
So I turn toward the teeth and tools
And work away the weary hours
While finches flit away outside like fools.
"Not fair!" I feel, they ought to offer
Something to share with the wide, wide world
Beside feathers and fluffy baby birds
And watching their weathered wings unfurl.
The grump grows in my heavy heart
As I wish I were the one with wings
And gripe and groan to stay inside
In dark desire for sun and shiny things.
Depression deepens as this day repeats
And my heart forgets the fluffy hope
Of bobbing birds and greening grass,
So in my murky mind I meander and mope.
But an idea imagined stirs my stinking soul
Of beautiful birds who do not spin or spade:
Gracious God cares for them and gives them goods
For peepers are only a part of much He has made.
Therefore, then I, who breathe His breath
Can count more care than any bobbing bird,
For I, imagined in His image and engineered with élan,

Have His Holy Spirit and hide His Holy Word.
Thus darkness departs and roses return
And I sing the song of Spring again,
Whistling while I work and smiling down on smiles
As Sonlight shines and removes the rain.
For God is good and sends us Spring
To cheer our cold and heavy hearts
And by its beauty hands us hope,
And forms us in His family, a precious, priestly part.
That we may tend the terrestrial ball
And hear and hearken to babbling birds,
Storing Spring and granting grace
To amaze all who wonder at His Word.
~~Jarrod Brown, DDS, DWS, 7 May 2015

God's Word is a Flower

God's Word is a flower
That brightens our days,
That grows and enlightens
And shines on our way.

It's petals are pages
Full of wisdom and love
That spread kindness to all
As a peaceful white dove.

Its center is Jesus,
God's Son, the Lord of Lords,
Who came here and saved us
And loves us more and more.

Its roots are a foundation
For living: Salvation,
Extended to all
Yes, even every nation.

Its stem is the Spirit
The single, sole one
Who instills in us hope
And love for everyone.

God's Word is a flower
Never wilted or still,
With a message for all:
A pollinator, if you will.

~~Jarrod Brown, August 1985, age fourteen

RED LETTER EDITION

Ruby red rules for life

Emanating from the eloquence of our Savior

Demand our discipline and discipleship.

Love in every lovely line

Emits exacting explanations of grace,

Told by our terrific teacher and

Transcribed for us by talented

Essayists, engaged in expressing

Redemption's radical design.

Evidence of eternal emancipation,

Designed by our doting Dad,

Inspires us to inordinate exertions

To teach, preach and reach the multitudes

In our immediate sphere of influence,

Offering them omniscient, omnipresent, omnipotent God

Nailed to a cross, raised from the dead, and reaching out
to love us.

~~Jarrod Brown, DDS, DWS, 23 July 2015

The Man and the Dogwood Tree

The man walked up the hill
With his friends in tow,
Singing and laughing,
Heading to the garden ornamented
With olive trees and dogwood trees.

The man walked into the garden
And his friends went to sleep,
Snoring very loudly,
And he bowed to pray near the dogwood trees,
His brow dripping with sweat and blood.

The man stood up suddenly:
His friend had kissed him on the cheek,
Pointing him out to the armed guards.
And they dragged him down the hill,
Carrying a chopped down dogwood tree.

The man walked up another hill
And his friends were scattered,
Denying they ever knew him.
And he was nailed to a dogwood cross,
His body beaten and bloody.

The man was carried down the hill
And his friends were crying out,
Wondering what would happen next.
They carried him to another garden
To a tomb in the rock by a dogwood tree.

The man was gone from the tomb
And his friends yelled in amazement
Cries of "He is Risen! He is Risen Indeed!"
And Mary met him in that garden,
Weeping tears of joy that watered the dogwood tree.

The man went up in the clouds
As his friends looked on
Knowing that everything would be fine.
And they went back to the garden tomb
And picked cross-shaped flowers off the dogwood tree.
~~Jarrod Brown DDS DWS, 25 March 2015

It Has Been My Understanding

It has been my understanding
that the love of God is outstanding
to all that life has left out standing in the rain
that falls
on all of us big and tall, large and small,
and really, after all,
It is a free gift from the Father above
who has wrapped up this gift of love
in the Body and blood of His Son
who with the Dove ministers to us all
with His unending grace
That has no place in this world or space
but nonetheless has won the race over sin and the grave
that was all the rave of Satan and his bunch
but not a fave of the God who rose
from the Cave and gave us life,
Which is never-ending as the Wife of the Christ
Who has ended the strife and the cut of the knife that
pierced His side, pouring out for us His Great Love.

~~Jarrod Brown, DDS, DWS, 29 February 2016

Fourteenth Anniversary

A surreptitious casual glance became a lifetime of looks.
A simple note became hours and then years of
conversation.
A concert became decades of beautiful music.
A lunch date became many meals together at the same
table.
A winter romance sprung into a May wedding and many
anniversaries.
A Hawaiian honeymoon began eons of special stories
and perfect pictures.
A pain of a child lost became two sons who enliven our
hearts and spirits.
A deep depression and darkness awoke to Sonshine and
laughter.
A job together became determination to survive and
succeed.
A job apart became thankfulness and gratitude to those
we serve.
A realization of family responsibility became hope,
peace, joy and deeper love.
A passion became a partnership and a powerful bond
that God still designs.
A pair became a couple.
A couple became one flesh.
A love became a lifetime.
And I will not let it go.
~~Jarrod Brown DDS, DWS to my wife Lisa Tunnicliff
Brown, for our 14th Anniversary, 19 May 2015

For My Lisa Jo

Side by side we walk together
Your hand in mine, fingers entwined,
Not only along this lane
But through the all the byways of life.
When I gave my heart to you
I had no idea how my world would change:
Loneliness abandoned,
Lovelessness reversed,
Languishing over.
Your care for me proves the love of God
And his promise to never leave or forsake.
For you have given the truth of your heart,
The beauty of your soul,
The industry of your hands,
The sensuality of your touch,
And shown me that two committed hearts
Can truly complete God's creation.
No matter what I had designed in my head,
He outpaced me in His thought of you.
For no one else could accept me,
Appreciate me,
Assist me,
Amaze me,
Or astound me as you, my love.
I praise you in all His creation as
More beautiful than roses,
 More artful than song,
More desirous than riches.
After the salvation I have in Christ,

The salvation of my life
In my marriage to you
Shines above all things.

Remembering our wedding day is joyful,
And many more occasions I pray we will have,
But looking forward to more of you,
More of us,
Is more wonderful than my words can express.

~~Jarrod Brown, DDS, DWS, 17 January 2016

SWEETPEA acrostic

Sharing laughs and love together,

We are so blessed by God above.

Even in the dark times of our existence

Everlasting love from above

Takes away the sting and makes us smile.

Peace is ours because we found

Each other and Him.

And nothing can put us asunder.

~~Jarrod Brown DDS DWS, 21 April 2015

In Memoriam

White marble rises from the top of stair,
Giving the place an almost holy air,
Especially as soldiers passing by
Pause their steps with naught a sigh.
A nameless comrade lies entombed,
Killed by warring factions' wound
And revered in place, by all who see,
For all who died to make us free.
Red, white, and blue upon the wreath
Salute the lads lying underneath
The sacred soil of battlefields,
Of cemeteries, and foreign shields,
Who gave their lives unselfishly
That their families might all be free.
We remember and regard with pride
Those men and women who have died
And we who live must carry on
To joyfully sing dear Freedom's song
That those who come behind us may
Enjoy each bright and sunny day.
Within our borders safe and sound,
America's heartbeat can be found:
If we but love, and care and pray
For each neighbor day by day.

~~Jarrod Brown, DDS, DWS, 16 January 2016

The Forest Floor

Sunshine yellow
Leafy green
Make bright puddles
On the forest floor.
Bouncing breeze
Wafting wind
Make trees dance
Above the forest floor.
Raucous robins
Calling cardinals
Make beautiful song
Above and upon the forest floor.
Circuitous paths
Trails untaken
Make me curious
About the forest floor.
Crunching cones
Snapping twigs
Make sneaking impossible
On the forest floor.
Glassy glimmers
Swinging doors
Make interesting outposts
On the forest floor.
Forgotten pews
Crooked crucifixes
Make dejected decorations
Above the forest floor.
Bell tolling
Bats scattering
Make surprising signals
Above the forest floor.

Wrecked headstones
Ruined tombs
Make family remembrances
Upon the forest floor.
Silent tears
Thoughtful smiles
Make me linger
On the forest floor.
Lives lived
Heavenly hopes
Make inspirational purpose,
And I leave the forest floor.

~~Jarrod Brown, DDS, DWS, 26 May 2015

3 Summer

An Antique Airplane

An antique airplane aims across my attic
And I wink and wave while he wings that way.
In turn, he wiggle-waggles the wings
And defies death and duty to dazzle my day.
Across a cloudy sky he climbs
And leisurely loops along his lofty lane.
Oh wow! I wish I were within
That amazing aeroplane!
But I am but a boy below,
My stems stuck to sandy shore,
Wishing awhile the waves awash
I were above in the air I adore.
So back up beachheads to bunk I bounce
Again aloft to the attic arise
So to see the seagulls and stars
And gladly give back the glider's goodbyes.

~~Jarrod Brown, DDS, DWS, 10 March 2015

Evening Dance
A cluster of diamonds flung upon a velvet backdrop,
overhanging the gentle roll of waves and white foam
becomes the evening dress of creation.
Twinkling lights from distant spheres and
shooting of stars across the expanse of darkness
invite me to the dance that has continued for millennia.

I am alone in the blackness with only my thoughts
to serve as my dancing companions. And yet,
I hear the song of so many others near and far.

There are those who dance among the stars
And those who serve the greater good by polishing up
The silver of the orbs that bring us nighttime joy.

There are those who skip across the pounding waters
or descend to the deeps to view the heavens through
a moving, bubble-filled lens,
yearning to be a part of the heavenly ball.

And there are those of us caught between the two veils,
Staring up and out and down and contemplating
who gave or rather why we have been given,
this privileged invitation.

All of this splendor, and music, and movement
draws us wallflowers to the center of the ballroom
That we may join in and find ourselves
dancing in the arms of the Creator.

~~Jarrod Brown, DDS, DWS, 22 November 2014

How You Love Us

You are King of the Universe, Almighty God,
You created the world with the words of Your tongue,
And you love us.
You spread out all the stars in the canopy of space,
You designed every member of Your human race,
And You love us.

We split the atom but You split all time;
With the cry of a baby you paid for our crime,
For You loved us.
With every step up the hill you forgave every blow,
And even death on the cross couldn't keep you below,
For You love us.

And your Spirit is here and we give You away
With each deed that we do and each word that we say,
And the tired and the poor and the needy all say,
"How He loves us!"

You love us so much Father, Spirit and Son
That the folly of man will be utterly done
And the fullness of life be restored to each one
When You love us...as You love us...
How You love us!

~~Jarrod Brown, DDS, DWS, 7 June, 2013, Holden
Beach, NC

JARROD BROWN, DDS, DWS

We Are Not Only, Simply Here

We are all not only, simply here.
We have a purpose, though we may not know what.
We wonder at it: That is why we peer
Through the universe of God, to find what?
The mystery of nature and its seed,
The stars, the spectrum, and the planets strange,
The beauteous flower, the purpose of the weed;
All this God was able to arrange.
He set in the sky the sun to give light,
Which gives all his children good health.
And the moon He gave us to brighten the night,
Which destroys Lucifer's nocturnal stealth,
Though we lack knowledge, we needn't fear:
Because we are all not only, simply here.

~~Jarrod Brown, 21 October 1986, age fifteen

Hang On To Love

In this old house,
I used a blanket for a toga,
And I cried on Mema's shoulder,
And I lived another life.

In this old house,
I ate my weight in macaroni,
Played with Papa's copper pony,
And I introduced my wife.

The days in this house seemed like they would
never end,
But the day soon came when all the fun was done,
And we closed the door to paradise and we drove
away at last,
And we carried all our heavy hearts away...

Well that old house,
It's got a brand new family,
And they've planted a new oak tree,
And they're building a new life.

And that old house
Is full again of laughter,
And the owner's middle daughter
Will soon be a brand new wife.

The love in that house, it will never have an end
'Til the day that Jesus takes us all away.
And He'll open up paradise and show us all at last,
And He'll carry all our heavy hearts away...

So, until then...

Hang on to love,
Take care of family,
Put off the urgent,
Sing a new song.
Death comes to all in due time,
So carry real hope in your mind,
Live out real life
And hang on to love!
It's never too late
You can start today:
Hang on to love.

~~Jarrod Brown, DDS, DWS, 21 July 2014

Reepicheep's Prayer
Guiding me from shining shore
Across the waves, the foaming waves
To wade knee-deep through lilied seas,
I hear your cry, Emperor's Son, in me.

To ride straight up that final wave
And see your hills so tall and green
Is the greatest wish of my tiny heart.
I pray, High King, this wish impart:

That I might be ever at your side
A blade in hand to serve you ever,
It is all the honor I dare observe
No matter what, my faith's preserved.

Just one small matter for your thought,
Regarding my honor once again:
This tail of mine's a bit too short,
I'd love the long and sweeping sort.

But, alas, though you have healed
That part of me that once was severed
I carry deep a scar inside
For almost losing faith to pride.

So in this coracle I come
Seeking rest and waters sweet.
Receive me, Lion, with velveted claw,
For I draw near in deepest awe.

For you created all I know:
This world of magic, dwarves and sword,
But I care no more for any one of these:
I long only now for your perfect peace
  ~~ Jarrod Brown, DDS, DWS, 24 January 2014

For My First Son

Today is a new day.
This is the first day I can call myself a daddy
Because now I know you are out there somewhere.
My child, the joy of our love,
Your mother and I have been waiting for you,
Patiently waiting,
Far longer than we care to remember.
Sometimes we wondered if you'd ever arrive
And sometimes we just about gave up.
Then again we would wonder how you would arrive
Would you come the "natural way,"
Or would you come by way of another lady's life?
God has the higher plan
And He is in control.
And just as He planned for that other Baby to arrive
By way of another Lady's life
So He has ordained your path to us.
So forever when I think
Of the miracle of your coming to us
By way of another life
I will always think of the Life
That came to us by way of another miracle.
Your life and His life are so intertwined,
I wonder what path you will travel now.
But that is not my concern
God has the higher plan
And He is in control.
For now I will love you
And show you His Love
Through constant prayer
Because now I know you are out there
Somewhere.
~~Jarrod Brown, DDS, 14 December 2005

Happy Birthday

Celebrate
The day you met the world--
Or did the world meet you?
Celebrate
With friends and family
Who give your everyday meaning.
Celebrate
The day your mother's pain
Melted into true love's smile.
Celebrate
The gleam in Daddy's eye
That became your spark of life.
Celebrate
The Father God who knew you,
Formed you in Mother's womb.
Celebrate
The relationship He offers
In the person of His Son.
Celebrate
The Spirit's work in your heart
And the works that flow from your hands.
Celebrate
A life of hope, peace, joy and love
And all the fulfillment it brings.
Celebrate
Defeats, losses, hurts, and pain
For they are the lessons that make you feel alive.
Celebrate
For you are you, uniquely you,
What will this year mean?

~~Jarrod Brown, DDS, DWS, 17 January 2016

Mother

Mother is my oldest friend
Whose own life she gave to lend
That I might grow to healthy be
In her loving care to learn to see
All the wonders God planned for me
Before the creation of the sea.

Mother was my very first teacher
Before my tiny hands could reach her
That I might learn the love of God
And all the beauty above the sod,
And show respect to those quite odd,
And meet a stranger with smile and nod.

Mother shaped her little man
With morals and with games so grand.
She taught me how to cook and clean,
And showed me fighting was too mean,
And introduced great books to glean,
And told me Jesus washed me clean.

Mother stood behind me grown,
A greater help I'd never known.
She taxied me to school and fun,
And cheered so loud when awards were won,
And dropped me off for my college run,
And cried to Father, Spirit, Son.

Mother's name has changed these days
As grandsons sing their Mimi's praise
And taxi runs begin anew,
And Jesus' plan is mentioned, too,
And little boys learn, and play, and do.
My Mother's legacy is glue
That holds our family forever true.

~~Jarrod Brown, DDS, DWS, 5 February 2016

Pentecost

Empty room, empty hearts
Sweltering heat, stifling air,
And no one knew quite what to do.
In prayer and in silence
They waited,
Because He had told them to.
When hope seemed gone,
Joy appeared crushed,
Love had flown,
And peace was nowhere to be found,
A wind began to move
Where all doors and windows were closed.
Could it be true?
Could His promise be fulfilling itself?
In tongues of flame,
Hope returned.
In voices before unknown,
Joy spilled out.
In the streets,
Love returned,

As thousands listened and were amazed.
God had loved them,
God had come down,
God had died,
God had resurrected Himself,
God had returned Home.
And in His place,
The Comforter came,
And peace began to spread,
Filling empty hearts,
Overflowing them with the Word of Truth.

~~Jarrod Brown, DDS, DWS, 5 January 2016

The Senses of Driving

The rushing of the river
The leaning of the lindens
The sunlight in the sky
The dance of the ducks
The gaggle of geese
These are the pictures of my drive to work.
The cacophony of cars
The honking of horns
The banging of brakes
The pounding of potholes
The ticking of traffic
These are the sounds of my drive to work.
The stink of a skunk
The ether of exhaust
The airiness of air freshener
The cologne of coffee
The mustiness of moss

These are the smells of my drive to work.
The smoothness of the steering wheel
The stiffness of the shifter
The action of the accelerator
The aching of my arthritis
The hurting in my head
These are the feelings of my drive to work.
The savor of my Starbucks
The vileness of my vitamins
The retching of my reflux
The cherry of my Chap-stick
The bitterness of my boredom
These are the tastes of my drive to work.
~~Jarrod Brown, DDS, DWS, 13 May 2015

Fourth of July

Red, white and blue
Flags and banners
Cannon and fireworks
Brighten up the air and sky
As the parade passes by.
A float in the shape of the Declaration
A Cryer reading the Constitution
A band playing the Anthem
"America the Beautiful" on every tongue
See how Freedom's song is sung.

But for every freedom there is a price:
War, pestilence, famine, dearth
Lord, bring us peace and unity

Among our family here on earth.
For all the poor, slaves to want
Bring wealth, health, home and hearth.
For all the ill, those facing death,
Bring hope, healing, and heaven's best.
Free us all from evil's trap and scatter Satan's nest.
Ring the bells of liberty
Sing out the freedom song
Let America stand as a beacon of hope
Standing together, shoulder to shoulder,
Against every bomb, and snare, and boulder,
Working out the hope of ages:
Godly worship from Godly pages.

~~Jarrod Brown, DDS, DWS, 14 December 2015

FREEDOM acrostic

Fear no longer has control of my life.
Redemption is at work in my heart:
Every shadow is expelled by His light.
Every moment He does his part:
Deepening our relationship,
Opening my eyes to His Truth,
Making me into the man He created me to be.

~~Jarrod Brown DDS, DWS, 5 August 2015

Driftwood Beach

Skeletons of trees litter the beach
Their corpses torn down from the cliffs
By that demon Erosion.
Bleached by the saline spray
Stripped of their skin and bare
They stretch their arms to each other and the sea
Searching for strength to upright their roots.
Some make it to the waves
Waving their body arms about
As they are dragged into the deep.
Those that remain lodged in the sand
Shake hands with others
Who have suffered the same fate
Whilst stretching out on the balmy beach.
Finding their fate quite firm
And their roots rather rickety
They slumber on the shore
Resigned to their ruinous repose.
~~Jarrod Brown, DDS, DWS, 24 March 2015

Alphabetical Alice

Alice aimlessly ambled among aromatic azaleas
Admiring ample amounts of amaryllis and asters
Arranged alphabetically along avenues and alleyways.

Blooms busted beautifully beside borders,
Bulbs brought bright blushing blossoms,
Bees buzzed busily, breezes blew, and bugs balanced.

Concealing clandestine courses, creeping carefully,
Conifers crowned with cones covered the celestial
corona,
Causing creepy corridors of continuing countryside.

Down deepening darkness, dappled dirt
Dug by daring, deft denizens of the deep Dean,
Diverts deliberation down and diverges devotion to
desired dahlias.

Every evening, each evergreen and edelweiss emanate
Essences evoking eau-de-toilette and even elegant
extracts,
Encouraging an emotional effect that eases edginess.

Flowers float fleetingly, fading and flimsy, forcing
falling.
Fluffy feathers fly finches forward and find family
feeding in ferns.
Frothing fountains flow frantically, feelings of
forgiveness follow.

Growing gloriously, gardens of glistening gardenias and
gladiolas
Give graceful grounds and grasslands glowing garlands,
Guiding guests to guess those grooms getting glued to
girlfriends.

Hiding hungrily here in heavy hedges, hedgehogs and
hares
Hollow holes in hemlock and herbs, hunting harriedly,
Hovering in hopes of healing hunger and then heading
home.

Iridescent irises imitate individual icons of indigo.
Intimate inklings of intelligent intention are illustrated
intensely.
Imagination increases, inducing insight to immortal
influence.

Junipers, jonquils, jasmine and Johnny Jump-ups
Jinglingly jiggle their jaundiced jabots
Jockeying for Jesus to join their joyfulness.

Kindergarteners kiss kindly kings in Kampuchean
kaftans.
Kidding around as kites keep kicking up.
Klutzily, knights in kilts knit knickers for knaves.

Lazily, larks lilt lightly aloft,
Licking lemons and luscious limes,
Looking lustfully for lovely little ladybugs.

Miracle Monet makes a matted mess,
Mashing melons into murky mugs,
Mixing muted magentas and marvelous mauves.

Naked nuts nip the noggins of naughty newts
Noticing Newton's notion needs no notary,
Now that nagging nuisances annihilate their noodles.

Opossums ogle other organisms oddly
Opining obliquely that "ordinary is obnoxious,"
Overlooking their own overwhelming oddities.

Peonies, pansies, and poppies proliferate,
Packing the patch with pulsating pigment,
Popping the peepers of probing passersby.

Quite quaintly, a quilting Queen
Quits her quackery and quickly queries,
Quenching the quest for quiz questions.

Rats reveling in reckless rioting
Reveal the ruinous remnants of their rampaging,
Running 'round risking radical retribution.

Spiders spin, snakes slither, and skunks stink,
Scaring socialites and scattering their soiree,
Spilling spaghetti and sweetmeats, soiling their suits.

Tomatoes, turnips, taro, and tarragon
Trim the trails of the train tracks.
Traveling tramps treat themselves to the tender tastiness.

Unaware of its ugliness, a urial upends an umbrella
Upon an undulating unicorn under an upturned umiaq.
Unrepentant, it urgently unties another and upchucks.

Very vibrantly, vines of various violets
Vastly velour the vista in vivid velvets.
Vandals' violence vanishes and victory is vaunted.

"Why such wild and wooly wishes
Wring my wizened wits?" she wonders.
"Where in the wide world will the wind whisk me?"

Xanthic xenon expressed in exit exhibits
Express an exotic paroxysm to exit this excellent exurb,
Exiling her excuses to express her vexation of this
existence.

Yearning to yell and yodel for Yolanda,
She yields to a yak and yatters about yellow,
Yirring at the yak she yelps and then yawns.

Zesty zebras zip past and zap her zest.
Zoning, she zooms to zombiland.
Zzzzzzzzzzzzzzzzzzzzzzzz.....

Alice asleep.
Alice awakes.

~~Jarrod Brown, DDS, DWS, 29 April 2015

4 Fall

Fall is Here
First frost
First fog
Fall is here.
First zip of sweater after
First nip of chill
Fall is here.
"Where are my gloves?
Where is my hat?
What is that white stuff?
Will it get on the cat?
Why did our summertime have to go away?"
"I don't know, Son, but Fall's here to stay."

First fire of the furnace
First visible breath of the year:
Fall is here.

~~Jarrod Brown DDS, DWS, 19 October 2015

AUTUMN FALLS acrostic
All our summer greens are turned to orange,
Umbers, browns, and golds line the way,
Trees bloom with the crisp, cool air
Under the blue sky that often turns grey.
Meadows are full, for the harvest has come,
New wine, pumpkins, wheat and the mums.
Feathery leaves flit toward the ground;
Aviary nests can hardly be found.
Little sun above shortens our days,
Lengthens our nights, but still gives God praise.
Softly the winter comes, and color fades to grey.

~~Jarrod Brown, DDS, DWS, 15 September 2015

Friday Night Lights
Hotdogs steam
Crowds convene
Stadium fills
ROTC drills
Anthem played
Flag raised
Hands shaken
Sides taken
Ball kicked
Receiver picked
Downs scored
Cheers performed
Goal crossed
Pompons tossed

Victory won
Alma mater sung
Mighty shout
Lights out
Another week
All repeats.

~~Jarrod Brown DDS, DWS, 22 September 2015

Friends

So many times the Lord has blessed
Each time in a new and different way
But every time He reaches out
He sends a new friend my way

They come from different places
Some near and some far away
And some come only for a visit
And some come in my heart to stay.

Some have nothing in common
And some could not be more alike
But each and every one of them
Is precious in His sight.

For He brought them out of darkness
To shine light upon my way.
He brought them to a broken heart
In need of help that day.

Each one He gave a special gift
That only we two could share
A time, a place, a common goal
A bond that He placed there.

Many of them have come and gone
Some I have with me now
Yet there are those who had their day
And walk with Jesus now.

But all of them embrace my heart
Each memory is clear
For every time that our lives touched
The Lord Himself was near.

~~Jarrod Brown, DDS, 18 October 2005

Autumn is the Mellow Time

Autumn is the mellow time
For resting up from labors done,
For cleaning up the summer fun,
And planning ahead for winter's clime.

It's colored leaves and pumpkins carved,
Backyard fires on coolish nights,
Watching bands under Friday lights,
And seeing healthy lawns grow starved.
It's brisk, wet walks on windswept days,
Scouting troops and popcorn sales,
New television fairy tales,
Bumpy hayrides and the old corn maze.

But when the tinted foliage falls
And cold obscures the summer sun
It's not the end of all our fun,
For winter's coat enchants us all.

Yet before the piles of snow can climb,
There's time for turkey, yams, and pie,
A quilt and cup of steaming chai,
And looking family in the eye,
And praising God, who with a sigh,
Created seasons on land, in sky,
And sent us trees in ginger dye,
Knowing He could catch our eye,
For Autumn is the mellow time.

~~Jarrod Brown DDS, DWS, 21 September 2015

CINDY MORGAN BROUWER acrostic

Creek beds and hollows in the hills beckon me.
I must go and write the music that fills my heart.
Never will I neglect this gift that God has given:
Day after day my soul resonates with His song.
Years have come and gone, and I still hear His voice.

Many times I have felt the weariness of a traveler
On the road, in the air, sharing His Good News.
Roaming my mind are all the people His music has touched:
Good people that have brought joy to my life.
And there are the great memories of family and friends,
Near and far, that have taught and encouraged me to write and
sing.

But greater still are the times I spend in the arms of love God
prepared for me
Relaxing and refreshing with laughter, and home, and our
children.
Out of their presence I am not the real me,
Unless I focus on the Father who made them and made me:
We are all family in Him first and foremost.
Even as I sing and write and proclaim His Name, fear will not
harm me…
Redeemer lives in me and I will forever praise the King.

~~ Jarrod Brown DDS, DWS, 2 December 2014 and dedicated
to my friend and fellow writer, Cindy Morgan Brouwer.

'Tis Time to Gird My Tartan On

'Tis time to gird my tartan on
And perch my old Glengarry
Pluck a feather from the cock in the yard
And nick my clan badge to carry.

Aye then we march the road to Kirk
And taste the salt-brine air
Feel the chill beneath our kilts
And realize the cold of knees so bare.

In the old stone kirk
An altar waits for family plaids
As pipes and drums lead down the aisle,
The Saltire is carried by two wee lads.

We remember those who wore no kilt,
Oppressed on every side.
Ere Cromwell's time to present day
We thank God clans abide.

We thank St. Andrew who followed Christ
And set our glad example
To follow the Lord up highland moors
E'en though our faith be trampled.

For following Christ is an arduous path
For Scot and English too,
Wee men are we and women folk
Who give His daily due.
For we are nothing outside His clan,
Like sheep upon the moors,
But folded in our tartaned Kirk
He loves us all the more.

We thank Thee, God, for Scotland brave
For Bruce and Stewart, too
May we give Thee our honest praise
As Thou hast given You.

~~Jarrod Brown, DDS, DWS, 14 December 2015

All Hallows Eve

Holes in trees
Where leaves should be
Show clearly to me
A house down the street
Where in the later Spring
I cannot see a single thing
For leaves and blossoms bring
A kind of privacy screen.
So now I see the spooky sight
Of children dressed in green and white
Coming down their drive a fright
In dreadful costumes that glow at night.
And through the open oaken branches
I catch in surreptitious glances
A monster runs, a skeleton dances
And many a horse and pony prances.

For this is that exciting night of year
Where even little children forget to fear
The floating of ghosties in the air so clear
So they can draw the candy near
And run back home right down the street
And tell all the goblins that they meet
Which houses are decorated so neat
And give out all the bestest treats.
And as the moon begins to wane
They run back down the street again
And enter the house with all their gain
As softly it begins to rain.
All Hallows Eve is over and done
And scary monsters (all for fun)
Are put away for a trip 'round the sun
When leafy boughs again are none.

~~Jarrod Brown DDS, DWS, 19 October 2015

The Face of Christ

The room was hot
The long hallway was cold
The room smelled of sweet perfume
The long hallway was filled with antiseptic vapors.
But there she sat,
A bright white smile beneath her snowy hair,
That belied the pain hugging her hips and back.
Our visit with her,
Filled with laughter and cherished memories,
Was interrupted by her churlish neighbor,
Whose smile had evaporated from her mind.
Instead of fond memories,
She only remembered that she needed to eat, asked for
dinner,
And when a few minutes had passed,
She asked for her dinner again.

With age comes many different challenges:
Bodies that betray us,
Minds that lose their hold on memories,
Families that are too busy to come near,
Or families that no longer walk this sphere.

But age does not strip us of our humanity,
The forgetfulness of the younger does not negate us.
The latter years can overflow with those who love us
Or bereft of anyone to love at all.

When we are old, our worth has not changed.
The price Jesus paid for us has not decreased.
When we are aging, we are moving closer to God,
But we are often further away from our families and
friends.

So as the year turns old,
Let us remember those who are older,
Not just during the season of light,
But every season of the year.
Show them love,
Glean their wisdom,
Meet their needs,
And let them remember the reason they were created.

While you visit there,
Check your eyes in the glass:
You might just see the face of Christ.

~~Jarrod Brown, DDS, DWS, 26 November 2014, in
honor of Mrs. Stuart Walton

All Saints

In our hearts their memories lie
A picture, a moment, a chocolate pie
All those things that made them ours
Never leave, but fill our hours.
For the lives they led to us revealed
All the things this world conceals:
The love of Christ, His peace and joy,
The hope for every girl and boy.
With all the endless ages of man
Our saintly ancestors stand,
A cloud of witnesses to watch
And cheer us on our lifelong march,
That we the path of endless light
Might follow on, fight the good fight,
And finish well the holy race
And at the end to see His face,
And share with them eternal time
That with Jesus Christ our hearts entwine,
Never again to spend life apart,
But living together within His heart.
And once the heavenly choir is joined,
We'll sing the prayer the Master coined,
And in everlasting praise with Spirit and Son,
"Our Father God, Thy will be done."

~~Jarrod Brown, DDS, DWS, 17 January 2016

Gone, Never Forgotten

Gone, never forgotten
Alive in me
Down in my heart of hearts
You drew me with love
Filled me with hope
Even in the deepest, darkest parts.
Your acts of praise
Made the life of this little boy,
All grown up
But still your child,
Living life through God's joy.
I learned through your example
Sometimes great,
Sometimes not,
But all the while you showed me
That it is God, and not the world,
That completes my empty Spirit spot.
The greatest of grandparents,
A father I did not fully appreciate,
A family that will never cease,
You live in my mind and heart,
You live in your heavenly reward,
You live, as I will then, in eternal, perfect peace.

~~Jarrod Brown, DDS, DWS, 26 February 2016

THANKSGIVING acrostic

Thankful again
He has brought us through
Another year together,
Nested snugly in our wonderful home,
Knowing that there are others
Suffering alone, without shelter or food
Going about their lives
Insecurely, intimidated by their sheer lack.
Victorious Lord, point us in their direction,
Infuse us with compassion and concern,
Needing to help others, that You might
Give us all the peace and love we crave.

-- Jarrod Brown, DDS, DWS, 26 November 2015
(Thanksgiving Day)

The Race For All Time (Christ the King)

The starting gates were opened,
As in time with the dawning of earth's first day.
From the pinnacle of Old Jerusalem,
Even to the day of the New City,
The White Horse and the pale Horse raced,
One with bow, the other with sword,
One sent forth to conquer,
The other sent forth to devour;
The Crown of Life won some to its source,
But Death was not without its victims.

As the middle of the race was reached
The circuit grew much more twisted and difficult,

With the White Horse and his band ahead
Pursued closely by the Pale One and all Hell with
him.
The attempts by the Archer at an early victory
We're sliced down by the evil swordsman.

When the race was finally ended
And the victory finally won,
We found, to our approval,
That both opponents finished not.
That champion, the White Horse,
Our savior, our Lord,
Retained his mighty title
Over the evil, pale rider.

For when the race neared its end
And Jesus whispered, "It is finished,"
All Satan could do was watch in despair
From his fiery pit in chains.
As the victory was won
And all sin was consumed in his blood,
The white Horse, the Lamb,
Ascended to Heaven above,
At his Father's right hand to reign
In New Jerusalem:
The finish line, our final home.

~~Jarrod Brown, 21 September 1986, age fifteen

God's Paintbrush

God's paintbrush exploded
And overnight, drips of color
Fell from Heaven
And covered the trees.

Super scarlet, like Superman's cape,
Deepest Orange, like the rising sun,
Golden Yellow, like a delicious apple,
Plums and purples from His royal throne.

All these colored leaves
Remind us of the peace God brings
When we trust Him
And depend upon His grace.

Red drops of blood from His Son that fell,
Orange brilliance of Sonrise on Easter morn,
Golden crowns that we will lay at his feet,
Purple velvet with which He will wrap us on His lap.

Autumn makes us mindful of a story that ends
With Jesus' Triumph as King of Kings
And prepares us for the story to start again
With the birth of the King in Bethlehem.

~~Jarrod Brown, DDS, DWS, 28 October 2015

5 Winter Returns

Advent Acrostic (HOPE, PEACE, JOY, LOVE)

He came as promised a night long ago,
Only seen by those who truly believed.
People of every kind witnessed His birth,
Every one of them in need of a Savior.

Plans for our salvation were made before the world:
Each of us was in God's mind as He created.
All the sins that man chose for himself,
Christ chose to ransom,
Even with His very life.

Jesus came not to condemn, but to free us.
Over and over again the prophets told us,
Yet we did not believe.

Lying in a tomb, even then He loved us.
Opening the tomb, He loved us all the more.
Victory was His and thus ours, and
Easter and Christmas stand together, the celebration of
   His Life.

~~Jarrod Brown, DDS, DWS, 15 December 2014

ROOT OF JESSE acrostic

Rahab, Ruth, and Bathsheba,
Obed, Boaz, and David.
Of this line of Judah He came
To make us part of His family.

Out of the people of God
Faith springs eternal.

Jesus came to save
Everyone who was and came after
So that we might be grafted in,
Spliced into the vine of God's love.
Emmanuel the Gardener, root of all hope.

~~Jarrod Brown DDS, DWS, 18 December 2014

JARROD BROWN, DDS, DWS

ROSE OF SHARON acrostic

Rains of hope
On Judean hills
Spring up a rosy shoot:
Emmanuel has come.

Out of Bethlehem,
Faith has bloomed.

Silvery star shines,
Herders hear,
Angels sing.
Righteousness unfurls
On a straw bed.
Now salvation blossoms.

~~Jarrod Brown DDS, DWS, 17 December 2014

IMMANUEL acrostic

In our hearts
Messiah makes all things new,
Moving us ever closer to who we are created to be.
Angel told Mary that she would carry God's son,
Now we carry His peace in our minds and souls as well.
Unimaginable the joy that stirs us,
Extraordinary the hope that guides us,
Love Himself, God with us, has come to us to dwell.

~~ Jarrod Brown, DDS, DWS, 17 December 2014

CHRISTMAS acrostic

Christ came,
Heaven rang,
Religion-enslaved
Israel saved.
Savior matures,
Tree He endures.
Magi were right,
All won that night:
Shepherds, and Gentiles, and Jews.

~~ Jarrod Brown, DDS, DWS, 17 December 2014

Christmas By The Shore

Winter rain flings a fog on the shore of the sea.
Though I attempt to ascertain those ambling along the
edge,
I finally ferret out faint outlines of coated friends
And their furry, four-footed fellows on long red leashes.

Foam from the whipped-up waves slides along the sand,
Turning me to tumbleweeds in the Texas plains.
The miniature mittens of children
find the marshmallowy mess
And smear it on their jeans in the cold air.

Sand that is usually so sizzling in the summer sun
Seems icy against my sandaled feet and skin.
The scratch of sea shells and crab claws click on my legs
And the screech of seagulls fills my senses with sound.

Grey clouds over the green sea obscure
the often bright orb
That steams the shore for scores of sunbathers
seasonally.
The wild winds instead whisk us into
woolen wraps and warn us
That the time for hot chocolate and warm apple cider
 is close at hand.

Christmas by the shore shines strange and simpler, but
just as special.
Red leashes remind of Rudolph's red nose
and foam of Santa's soft beard.
Stretches of sand summon scenes
 of Three Kings scanning the desert sky
And grey clouds glow with the Glorias
of the heavenly host
Boasting of the birth of the Babe of Bethlehem.

~~ Jarrod Brown, DDS, DWS, 23 November 2014

Times Yet to Be

The tail-end of something wonderful:
A beautiful parade has passed us by.
Elephants and autumn and Epiphany,
Easter and Christmas and Fourth of July.
Every tender memory
Plucked and pressed and put away,
The sweet rose of family and friends,
Blooms again on New Year's Day.
In the midst of the chaos of life,
One thing has become clear:
Our relationship with Jesus
Should be the focus of our year.
For He is with us here and there,
Along every road and every bend,
Watching over, holding our hand,
Teaching our broken hearts to mend.
The Father of love our guide has been,
The Holy Spirit has lighted our way,
The Holy Word of God our text:
A faithful Rabbi in December or May.
His mighty Resurrection power
Has defeated all our various sins,
And we, now saints, forever stand,
In eternal victory with Him.
So come rejoice and sing with me,
Raise our voices to the One of Three,
A great year is gone, a great year we see,
With Christ we walk into times yet to be.

~~ Jarrod Brown, DDS, DWS, 21 January 2016

About The Author

Jarrod Brown, DDS, DWS is a practicing dentist and full-time theologian who has been writing since he was in Kindergarten. He resides in Danville, Virginia, with his wife Lisa, a Certified Public Accountant, and their two sons, Trevor and Nathan. He is a graduate of George Mason University, Virginia Commonwealth University, and The Robert E. Webber Institute for Worship Studies.

You may check out his book website at
www.doctorpoet.com
and his dental website at
www.danvillevadentist.com

www.ingramcontent.com/pod-product-compliance
Lightning Source LLC
Chambersburg PA
CBHW032028090426
42741CB00006B/767